MY FIRST
RECORDER
Ben Parker

Learn To Play
Right Away!

This Book Belongs To:

Author: Ben Parker

Editor: Alison McNicol

First published in 2013 by Kyle Craig Publishing

This version updated Dec 2014

Text and illustration copyright © 2013 Kyle Craig Publishing

Design and illustration: Julie Anson

Music set by Ben Parker using Sibelius software

ISBN: 978 -1-908-707-18-5

A CIP record for this book is available from the British Library.

A Kyle Craig Publication
www.kyle-craig.com

Contents

INTRODUCTION

Welcome to My First Recorder book!

The recorder is one of the easiest instruments to learn. Its size and simplicity makes it an easy instrument to get to grips with quickly, and many beginners will be playing their first tune within minutes. Many children learn recorder at school too, and because a recorder is a small, light and easy instrument to carry around, you can play and practice anywhere you like!

In this book we aim to give you your first simple steps to playing recorder, and hope you have tons of fun along the way! Also included in the book is a step by step guide to reading music.

 ## Practice

Like any skill, playing an instrument takes a lot of practice. Practicing more regularly for shorter lengths of time is more effective than practicing for an hour or so just once a week. The minimum amount would be around 15-20 minutes 3 to 4 times a week. The ideal amount would be 20 minutes a day, 7 days a week. Maybe set out a plan of your week and work out the best times to fit your practicing around the other things you do. The more your practice can become part of your weekly or daily routine the better.

Remember, little and often is best!

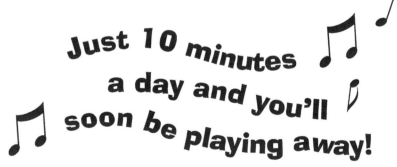

Just 10 minutes a day and you'll soon be playing away!

About The Recorder

The recorder is part of the woodwind instrument family. Recorders are mentioned in history as early as the late 14th century, but art and literature tells us that similar instruments were played much earlier in Medieval times.

Recorders were often used as part of ceremonies such as weddings and funerals. In the 18th century the orchestral members of the woodwind family took over from the recorder. Then in the 20th century the recorder's popularity grew again when it was used to help teach music to children.

There are a few different sizes of recorder. The most common at beginners level is the smallest one, the soprano recorder. This size recorder is also known as a descant recorder. This is the one you will be learning on.

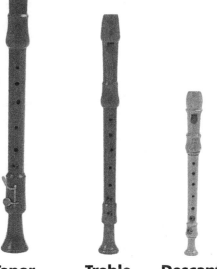

Tenor   **Treble**   **Descant**

The Instrument

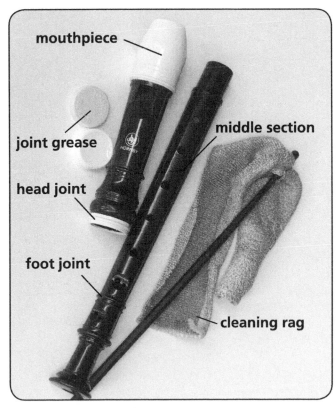

mouthpiece

joint grease

head joint

foot joint

middle section

cleaning rag

The recorder is made up of three parts, or joints, and a mouthpiece. The foot joint and the middle section on some recorders are fixed.

You may want to take your recorder apart to clean it. To do this, hold two of the joints and twist them apart. If the joints are stiff you can rub a small amount of joint grease on the connecting parts to allow the recorder to be pulled apart more easily in the future.

Do's and Don'ts

Do try and clean your recorder after playing — most recorders come with a 'mop' for this.

Do put your recorder back in its case after use.

Don't leave your recorder outside or next to a radiator. Extreme temperatures may damage it.

Don't bite or chew the mouthpiece!

How To Hold Your Recorder

Because the recorder is such a lightweight instrument it's just as easy to stand when playing as it is to sit down. Hold your recorder at an angle with your elbows pointing slightly outwards. Try to use a music stand to hold this book so your back is straight with your head up.

Fingers

Your right hand should always hold the recorder, whether the fingers are covering the holes or not. Start with your right hand thumb around the back of the recorder (where the 4th hole is on the front).

Now bring your left hand thumb around the back of the recorder over the hole and put your 1st (index) finger of your left hand over the top hole on the front.

Mouth

Put the mouthpiece of the recorder in your mouth between your lips (keep your teeth covered with your lips) and never bite the mouthpiece or touch it at all with your teeth.

Tonguing

Now you have everything in the right place try blowing into your recorder. Use the *'ter'* sound as you blow — this is called tonguing and helps you to use your tongue in the right way when playing.

Try blowing a few in a row to help you get the hang of it.

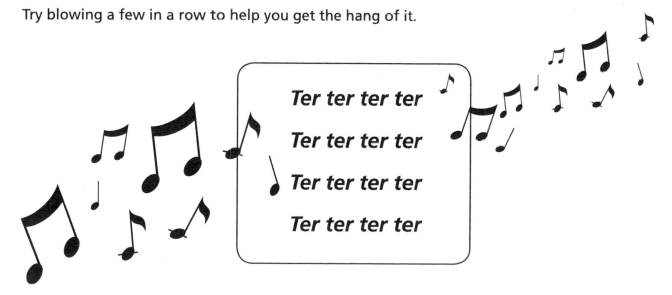

Ter ter ter ter

Ter ter ter ter

Ter ter ter ter

Ter ter ter ter

Knowing Your Notes

The notes on the music stave (see below) either sit in the spaces or on the lines. As notes go higher vertically on the stave they go higher in pitch. As they go lower vertically on the stave they go lower in pitch.

Notes in the spaces

F A C E

Notes on the lines

E G B D F

The note is in the space, man!

Every Good Boy Deserves Football!

Your recorder's lowest note is **C** (written as middle **C** on the piano but sounding 1 octave up) and the highest note of most soprano recorders is a high **D** above the stave. This is what is called the **RANGE** of the instrument.

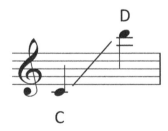

D

C

Music runs alphabetically from **A** to **G** and then starts again on **A**. When notes go above or below the stave we use **ledger lines** to keep track of how many spaces/lines down or up they are. So, the notes on your recorder run like this:

ledger line

C D E F G A B C D E F G A B C D

Other Musical Symbols

There are many symbols used in written music. Some are used to help us navigate our way around and some are used to give instructions along the way.

You will see the **Treble Clef** at the beginning of all recorder music. This tells us where the notes are to be played.

The **Time Signature** is an important sign at the beginning of any piece of music. It tells us how many beats to count in each bar. At a beginners' level it is only really important to look at the top number. This will tell you how many beats there are in a bar.

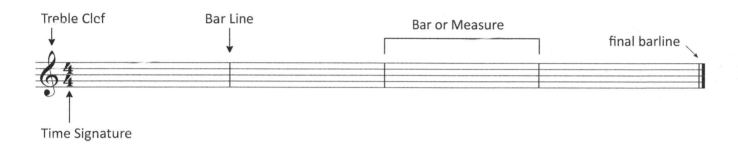

Notes and Note Lengths

Some notes last for longer than others. To show these different lengths notes look different according to their duration:

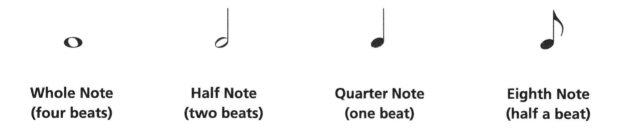

Whole Note	Half Note	Quarter Note	Eighth Note
(four beats)	(two beats)	(one beat)	(half a beat)

The Note B

Let's start by playing the note **B**. To help you with fingerings there will be a finger diagram for every new note that you'll learn. This will appear next to a mini stave showing the note in music.

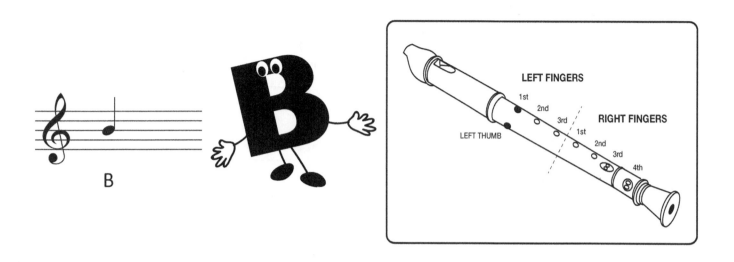

B

LEFT FINGERS
1st
2nd
3rd   RIGHT FINGERS
LEFT THUMB   1st
2nd
3rd
4th

To get you started let's '*ter*' (tongue) our way through the following simple tune. In the second and fourth bars you have a half note. **Remember to count 2 beats for every half note.**

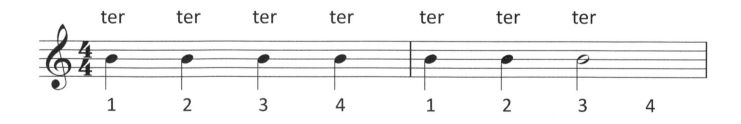

ter   ter   ter   ter   ter   ter   ter

1   2   3   4   1   2   3   4

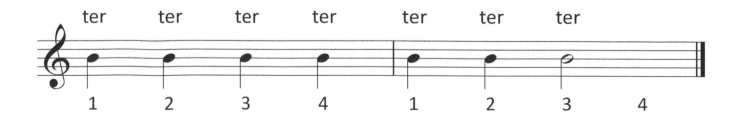

ter   ter   ter   ter   ter   ter   ter

1   2   3   4   1   2   3   4

Let's try another two pieces with the note **B**. These will have words written below to help you with the rhythms. Try reading the words first before you try playing the note **B** along to the same rhythm:

Let's Bake Cakes

Let's   bake   cakes   it's   such   fun

stir   stir   mix   mix   yum   yum!

Playing Football

Play - ing   foot - ball   all   day   long

watch   me   score   that   goal!

Quavers

So far we've only used whole notes, half notes and quarter notes. Our new note length is an eighth note. This is also known as a quaver. These last for half a beat. When counting eighth notes use **1 & 2 & 3 & 4 &**. This will help you with the rhythm.

Lets try our new note **A** with eighth notes.

The Note A

A

Scooting Fast

Watch me scoot-ing real-ly fast scoot-ing down the hill

Now let's try a mixture of **B** and **A** notes, **quarter** notes and **eighth** notes.

Tired Little Daisy

Tired   lit - tle   Dai - sy   go   to   sleep

tired   lit - tle   Dai - sy   sleep   sleep

The Breath Sign

The **breath sign** ✓ tells you where to breathe. Keep your eyes peeled for these — they will help you to be careful with your breathing. You can also breathe where there is a rest in the music too.

My New Kitten

Play - ing with my kit - ten is my favour - ite thing

play - ing with my kit - ten is such fun

13

The Note G

G

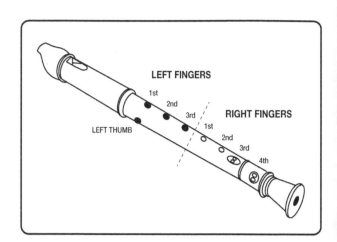

Now we have 3 notes we can play a proper tune.

Mary Had A Little Lamb

Repeat Marks

Sometimes you may want to play the same passage of music more than once. To save writing out that passage of music again we use repeat marks. When you see a closing repeat mark you either go back to the opening repeat mark or, if there isn't one, you go back to the beginning of the piece.

opening repeat mark   end repeat mark

Try the piece below. Note when you get to the end you have an end repeat sign. This means you should go back to the beginning and play the whole piece again.

Far From Home

 # 3/4 or Waltz Time

So far all of our pieces and exercises have been written with 4 beats to a bar. **4/4** is probably the most common time signature you will come across. The other time signature you will see a lot is **3/4** (three beats in a bar). Commonly known as **Waltz time,** it was also a popular dance in the late 18th century.

Dotted Notes

A dot next to a note tells us to lengthen the note by half again. So a dotted half note (or 2 beat note) is worth 3 beats. This comes in very handy in waltz time!

Try playing '**Ballet Dance**' and remember to count 3 beats to each bar. Don't forget to play the dotted half note for 3 beats.

Ballet Dance

Other Time Signatures

You can also have two beats in a bar. This is written as **2/4** and is often called **March time.**

Try playing the piece below in **2/4**.

On The March

The Note E

E

The Homework Blues

Rests

Rests tell us when *not* to play. Like notes, they last for different lengths of time. These different lengths are shown as different symbols:

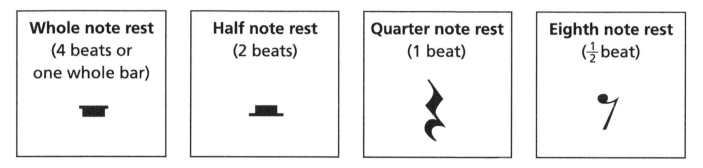

| **Whole note rest** (4 beats or one whole bar) | **Half note rest** (2 beats) | **Quarter note rest** (1 beat) | **Eighth note rest** ($\frac{1}{2}$ beat) |

Try playing the next piece and concentrate on your rests. This piece also features your new note **E**.

Taking A Rest

Now you've built up your knowledge on the recorder here are a few pieces featuring all your notes, musical symbols and rests. The pieces will get more difficult as you go through them. Try to play the new pieces slowly and speed up when you feel more confident.

Morning Sun

Watch out for the dotted quarter note in the next tune. Try and count through it using '**and or &**' for the eighth note. To help get used to these new note lengths, try clapping the rhythm first.

The Milkshake Song

Watch for the repeat section in this piece.

Creepy Crawlies

 # Ties

A **tie** joins two notes together— you only have to play the first note but it now lasts longer (its length + the length of the note it is tied to).

tie

Try this next piece. Watch your breathing because the tied notes will take a lot of breath to last as long.

All Sewn Up

The Note D

D

LEFT FINGERS

1st
2nd
3rd

RIGHT FINGERS

LEFT THUMB

1st
2nd
3rd
4th

'**Sing It Loud**' has an '**anacrusis**' or '**pick-up beat**'. This is the note right at the beginning of the piece that acts as an introductory note before the first main downbeat of bar 1. The last bar of the piece only has two beats to compensate for this.

Sing It Loud

Slurs

A slur is a curved line and looks similar to a tie. It is used to join two different notes together so there is a smooth transition between them. To play two slurred notes, tongue the first note then change to the next note without tonguing again for the second note. One blow should cover both notes.

Try the following exercise slurring between the **A** and **B** notes. Use the tonguing indication written below to help you remember your tonguing for the two notes:

ter_____   ter_____   ter_____   ter

Long Ride Home

The Note C' (Upper C)

C'

Be careful with your tonguing when playing from **B** to your new note **C'**. Because finger 1 on your left hand has to come up you'll have to work extra hard on separating the notes.

Try this exercise first to get used to the change from **B** to **C'**.

Now try playing this piece. Make sure your slurred notes are nice and smooth.

Sail The Seas

To The Fair

In **'Story Time'** below we look at ***pushed*** rhythms. This is when some of your notes are played just before the main beat — often as an eighth note tied to the next note. This is where music can get it's **'groove'** from — it's ability to make you dance! See bar 2 for the first example of a pushed rhythm.

Story Time

Staccato

Staccato is when you play short and detached notes. The small dot below or above a notehead tells us to play the notes staccato. To play a staccato note use a '***tut***' sound rather than a '***ter***' sound for tonguing. This will help you end the note quickly.

tut   tut   tut   tut   ter   ter

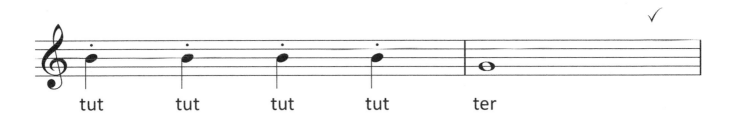

tut   tut   tut   tut   ter

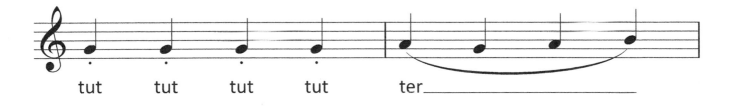

tut   tut   tut   tut   ter_____

tut   tut   tut   ter

The Note **D'** (Upper D)

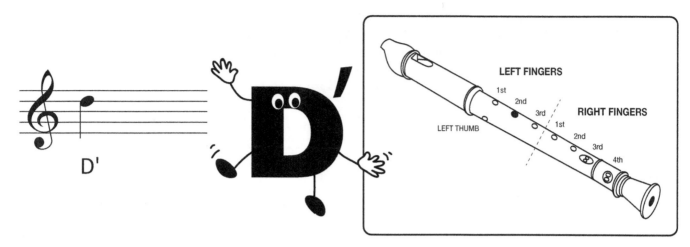

D'

Sound The Horn

 **Quiz**

Name that note!

- -

- -

- -

How many beats do each of these notes last for?

HALF/ONE/TWO/FOUR   HALF/ONE/TWO/FOUR   HALF/ONE/TWO/FOUR   HALF/ONE/TWO/FOUR

Can you write the correct note beneath each fingering diagram?

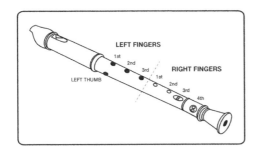

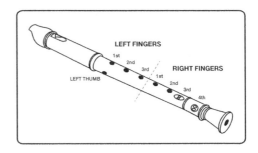

- -

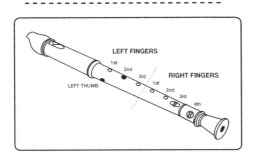

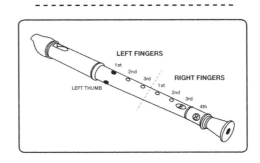

- -

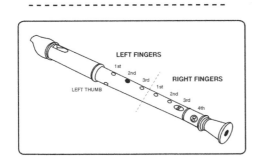

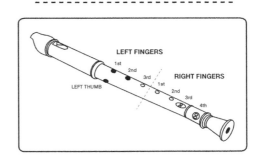

- -

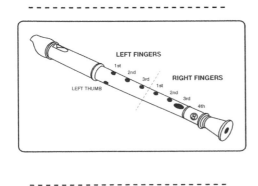

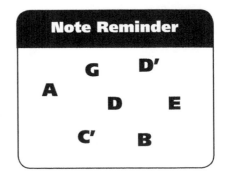

Note Reminder

G   D'

A   D   E

C'   B

- -

Quiz

Can you colour in the correct holes to cover when playing each note?

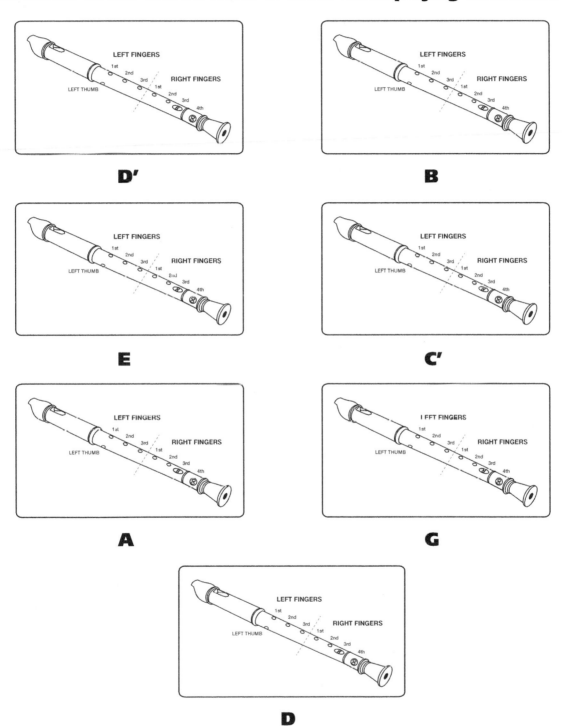

D'

B

E

C'

A

G

D

MORE GREAT MUSIC BOOKS FROM KYLE CRAIG!

 **How To Play UKULELE —** A Complete Guide for Absolute Beginners

978-1-908-707-08-6

 **My First UKULELE —** Learn to Play: Kids

978-1-908-707-11-6

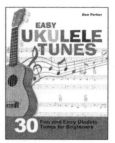 **Easy UKULELE Tunes**

978-1-908707-37-6

 **How To Play GUITAR —** A Complete Guide for Absolute Beginners

978-1-908-707-09-3

 **My First GUITAR —** Learn to Play: Kids

978-1-908-707-13-0

 **Easy GUITAR Tunes**

978-1-908707-34-5

 **How To Play KEYBOARD —** A Complete Guide for Absolute Beginners

978-1-908-707-14-7

 **My First KEYBOARD —** Learn to Play: Kids

978-1-908-707-15-4

 **Easy KEYBOARD Tunes**

978-1-908707-35-2

 **How To Play PIANO —** A Complete Guide for Absolute Beginners

978-1-908-707-16-1

 **My First PIANO —** Learn to Play: Kids

978-1-908-707-17-8

 **Easy PIANO Tunes**

978-1-908707-33-8

 **How To Play HARMONICA —** A Complete Guide for Absolute Beginners

978-1-908-707-28-4

 **My First RECORDER —** Learn to Play: Kids

978-1-908-707-18-5

 **Easy RECORDER Tunes**

978-1-908707-36-9

 **How To Play BANJO —** A Complete Guide for Absolute Beginners

978-1-908-707-19-2

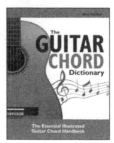 **The GUITAR Chord Dictionary**

978-1-908707-39-0

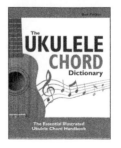 **The UKULELE Chord Dictionary**

978-1-908707-38-3

RECORDER NOTES CHART

✂ CUT OUT THE NEXT 2 PAGES AND PIN
TO YOUR WALL TO HELP YOU PRACTICE!

NOTES CHART

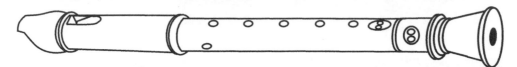

B

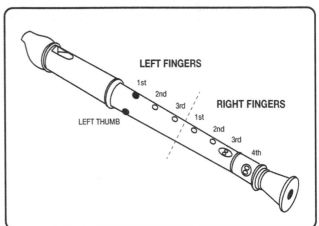

A

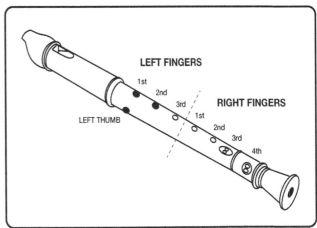

G

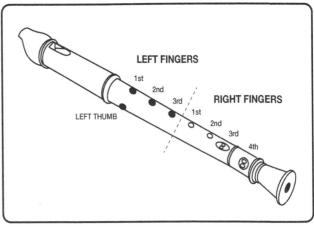

E

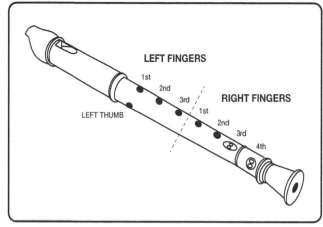

LEFT FINGERS
1st
2nd
3rd
RIGHT FINGERS
LEFT THUMB
1st
2nd
3rd
4th

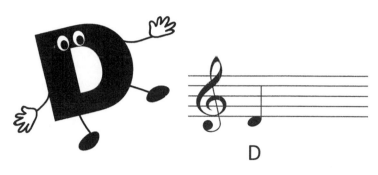

D

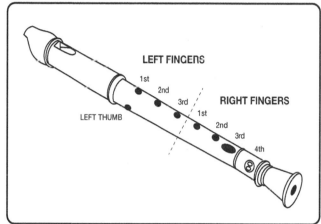

LEFT FINGERS
1st
2nd
3rd
RIGHT FINGERS
LEFT THUMB
1st
2nd
3rd
4th

C'

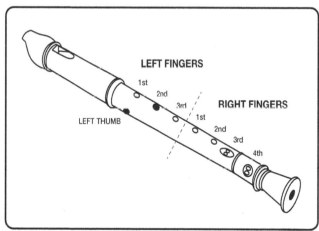

LEFT FINGERS
1st
2nd
3rd
RIGHT FINGERS
LEFT THUMB
1st
2nd
3rd
4th

D'

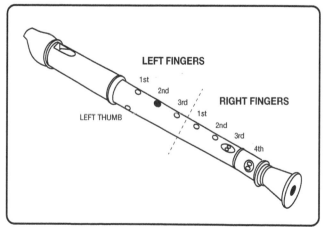

LEFT FINGERS
1st
2nd
3rd
RIGHT FINGERS
LEFT THUMB
1st
2nd
3rd
4th

Printed in Great Britain
by Amazon